Stormy Waters is invaluable to anyone who has experienced a significant loss. It provides a healthy perspective on grief and will leave the reader with compassion for others, practical means of dealing with bereavement, and a sense of hope. Life must go on.

Dr. Robert Puglia, psychologist

Stormy Waters motivated me to recall my experience working as a nurse in the intensive care unit, witnessing the grieving process of my patients as well as their families. Rosalie turned her pain to a purpose and illustrates that intense grief eventually turns to relief.

Connie Wuttke, RN

The death of anything that defines you as a person can be tragic, whether it's the tragedy of 9-11, changing jobs, losing a spouse, finding a lump, or just moving to a new city. As a librarian, I've seen many authors attempt to explore the dichotomy between death and life but very few, if any, have approached it with the earnest grace of Rosalie. This book will help those in the midst of heart-wrenching hopelessness work through their despair to see the bright rays of a new beginning.

Monika Sisbarro
librarian and former widow

This book is a lovely salute to a lost loved one and shows how helpless and courageous we, as the bereaved, can be.

Dr. Harry B. McCain
biologist and former widower

As a physician and surgeon, I often confront death and dying. Taking care of a disease is straightforward; taking care of the patient and family provides a far greater challenge. I thought I did both fairly well until my beloved mother died. *Stormy Waters* quietly, effectively, and most completely explores this indefinable period during which both body and spirit are overwhelmed. Rosalie leaves a glimmer of hope for us all.

Earl F. Jackman, DO, OBGYN

Death is universal; yet grieving and mourning are personal and introspective. Rosalie reveals an insightful account of her own journey transcending from shock and grief to hope and love. Her reflections are inspirational for anyone struggling to cope with personal loss.

Judy Pfennig
educator and widow

Stormy Waters is much more than eloquent words from a grieving author; it is a collaboration of feelings, experiences, tears, cheers, and fears. The author's journey is well defined and a familiar travel for all of us. She effectively illustrates how life's most precious commodity—mental, emotional, physical, and spiritual health—heals with time and perseverance. Rosalie allows the reader to experience feelings and emotions freely not only within the words of text but also through the empty spaces between the lines. The take-home message, for me, is that we never have to be or really are alone. I look forward to more inspirational pieces from this author.

Mark Bartiss, MD, alternative medicine

Stormy Waters

From the Darkness of Grief to the Light of Hope

Stormy Waters

From the Darkness of Grief to the Light of Hope

Rosalie Stolinski Siciliano

Brown Books Publishing Group
Dallas, Texas

Stormy Waters
From the Darkness of Grief to the Light of Hope

© 2009 Rosalie Stolinski Siciliano

All rights reserved. No part of this publication may be used or reproduced in any manner whatsoever without written permission except in the case of brief quotations embodied in critical articles and reviews.

Interior illustrations by Rich Davis, MFA.

"Appropriate Expectations You Can Have for Yourself in Grief" reprinted by permission of Dr. Therese A. Rando.

Manufactured in the United States of America.

For information, please contact:
Brown Books Publishing Group
16200 North Dallas Parkway, Suite 170
Dallas, Texas 75248

www.brownbooks.com
972-381-0009

A New Era in Publishing™

ISBN-13: 978-1-934812-50-1
ISBN-10: 1-934812-50-1

LCCN: 2009932838
1 2 3 4 5 6 7 8 9 10

Dedicated to my remarkable daughters

Denise, Therese, and Cheryl

Acknowledgments

As we go through life, we are who we are. When tragedy hits, we become someone we cannot identify. During that time in my life, so many people indulged me with expressions of compassion, love, kindness, support, and care. These are the ones who held me up.

A gracious thank you to my girls, my blessings whom I cherish—Denise Walsh, Therese Fergus, and Cheryl Parker—who had to deal with their own emotions and grief from losing their loving father while also sustaining my sanity. They never left my side.

And to their wonderful husbands: Eddie Walsh, who lost his golf buddy and friend; Rich Fergus, whose hugs felt so good; and Rich Parker, who was so comforting.

To my grandchildren, every one of them; their simplicity and innocence bring joy to my heart: Jessica, Jonathan, and Kaitlyn Walsh; Heidi and Greta Fergus; Nicholas Semanchik (who had some real gems as to how and where Pop-Pop went); Micaela Semanchik; and Jake Parker.

Thanks to my brother, Tom Czulewicz, and his wife Dianne, who helped keep me going in so many ways I lost count. To Pricilla Lynch, who worked at Scholastic Books for years and proofread my first manuscript. Also to Jack Schneider, who lives in Maine and writes children books; he perused my first manuscript and gave me his input.

To Ann and John Osterburg, who adopted me when I moved next door, held buckets to catch all my tears, and led me in prayer. Also to Robin Sneddon, my friend and confidant, who picked up the load graciously and dealt with my daily ups and downs as I ranted and sniffled with the difficulties of accepting my loss. And to Jacque Rittereiser, who whispered gentle, sweet thoughts of wisdom to me with compassion and generosity.

There is a special place for Margie Thaler, with her tenderness and love, along with Millie Farenwald, my dearest friend and soul mate, who have both prayed with me and listened to all phases of my weeping, sorrow, pain, frustration, and supported my fervent desire to be centered with our *Lord*.

There are many special dear ones out there—my cousins, they know who they are, and so many friends and clients. Stan Bialomizy, your letter is a treasure.

Thank you to Jim Stovall for connecting me with Brown Books Publishing Group and for writing such a beautiful foreword.

Thanks to Rich Davis for being so willing to contribute to this project at such a late point in the process.

And finally, thank you to the staff of Brown Books Publishing Group, including Milli Brown (wise owner and team leader), Kathryn Grant, Dr. Janet Harris, Bill Young, Cathy Williams, Cindy Birne, Jessica Kinkel, and Jennifer Allen. My book would not be the remarkable product it is without each of you.

Challenge

By my mother, Julia Czulewicz

I challenge the wind
To the flight on the wing
To firmaments unknown and forgotten
For where the wind blows
The mighty wing shall soar
Beyond the distant horizon
High above the roaring sea
Thus my love, my faith aspires
I have but to think of thee.

I challenge the roaring sea
Its sanctums lie indisposed
Profound in its consistency
Forbidding – but to those who are bold
Age-old tales by salts retold
Of far-flung shores, of whitecaps ride
Upon the swelling of the tide
Endless, bottomless, the roaring sea
More so the depth of my love for thee.

Contents

Foreword xix
Preface................................. xxi
Introduction xxv

Past 1
  Remembering the Love 13
  The Touch of Joy 14
  Hear Me *Lord* 15
  A Timeless Love 16
  Fantasize.......................... 18
  Bond of Togetherness 19

Present............................. 21
  Prayer of Widows and Widowers...... 29
  The End Has Come................... 35
  Death.............................. 36
  Waves Wash Over Me................. 37
  What to Feel....................... 38
  Falling into Helplessness.......... 39
  Body Within........................ 40
  Links of Separation................ 41
  Confusion.......................... 42
  Breaking into Pieces 43
  Closing Down Inside 44

Lost in the Wilderness 45
Speaking into Silence 46
The Question? 47
Falling Apart 48
Forgotten 49
Stormy Waters 50
Stillness 51
Appropriate Expectations You
   Can Have for Yourself in Grief 52

Future 57
Alone, Alone, Alone Again 63
Time Is Passing Me By 64
Petition 65
Searching 66
He Touched Me... 67
From Sorrow to Stillness 69

A Fairy Tale Romance 71
One True Knight 73
Epilogue: There Is Hope 75
Afterword: A Faith-Filled
   Journey through Grief to Hope 81
Memories 87
About the Author 99

Foreword

Grief is something we all have experienced or will experience in our lifetime. The only people who never feel the grief of losing someone special are people who live in the human poverty of never having special people in their lives.

I have written a dozen books, but if I am known for any of them, it is the novel *The Ultimate Gift* and the subsequent movie from 20th Century Fox based on my book. In the movie, the character played by James Garner has died and left his grandson a legacy of lessons that Jason does not appreciate or value. At the end of the movie, Jason has learned the valuable life lessons his grandfather left him and only then does he experience grief for someone who has been gone over a year.

It was a wise man who posed the question whether it is better to have loved and lost than never to have loved at all. As painful as loss is, always choose love, as it makes life worth living.

In these pages, you are going to experience one woman's life and loss. She and I both hope that her pain will bring comfort to you now and in the future.

Jim Stovall
Author, *The Ultimate Gift*

Preface

I wanted to say that I don't know what the etiquette is for grieving, or if there even is one. Nevertheless, if there is an emotion, standard, or method for dealing with loss, I am not aware of it. When my husband died, it was very sudden—an aneurysm of the frontal lobe of the brain and then heart failure. I really don't know what happened to me after that. One thing is for certain—I didn't deal with it very well. My daughters and their husbands completely took over. With their fortitude, calm, and love, they managed to take care of all that was necessary and get ready for the funeral. However, from then on one would think I could handle what followed—I couldn't and didn't. All the papers, insurances, and forms to be filled out, people to contact, and bills to be paid were taken care of by them. One week after my husband died, I wound up in the hospital with a heart-related issue. If a letter, card, or flowers came, I found myself floundering and felt choked and frozen, unable to function the way

I would have normally. Even to go back to that time is very difficult—mainly because I don't have a memory for much of it.

I did continue to work, needless to say at a different pace. Whenever I had to look for something or do something related to my husband, I wound up crying and having to visit the ladies' room often, feeling sick. I felt that way for almost a year; undoubtedly, I was in shock. My girls had to sort through the mail and follow up with phone calls. There are times I still find myself wondering where I was mentally.

My awareness of the different physical and mental emotions I experienced is still amazing to me. Right from the onset of Ed's death, I knew he went home to be with our *Lord*. That was totally acceptable to my spiritual being. Everything else—the loss of him, missing him, and experiencing his absence—created a torrent of mirages that I felt then and experience still.

I often wonder how people who don't have dear close friends or children like mine survive. With their love and support, I continue forward. Only with our *Lord's* supreme power and constancy of grace, mercy, and love are the promises of survival.

Rosalie Stolinski
February 20, 2003

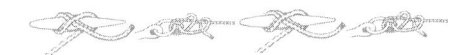

Away! We know the tears are vain,
That death nor heeds nor hears distress:
Will this unteach us to complain,
Or make the mourner weep the less?

—Byron

Introduction

My husband died on August 9, 2001, and as I reeled with devastation from that event, still dealing with the loss of my mother-in-law six months prior, the 9-11 tragedy occurred. My daughter Terri saw the second plane hit the World Trade Center on her way into work on Wall Street. She, too, felt the blow of it. With these incidents intertwined, my life became overwhelming and confusing. I started to assemble my feelings on paper, wanting to escape the sorrow and pain that I felt ruined me. This book is a summary of those feelings.

I believe there are many who mourn and are experiencing the same chaos of emotions I've gone through. Knowing that others feel this pain, I wanted to share these personal, psychological reactions I encountered in the hope of helping others heal. Through many highs and lows, and by the mercy and grace of *God*, I am functioning. I am not the same person that I was with my husband, and I recognize that I will never again be who I was with him.

As the tide ebbs and flows, so too did our life swing smoothly during the decades we shared—until the pendulum *abruptly stopped*.

— Past —

Are we not one? Are we not join'd by heaven?
Each interwoven with the other's fate?
Are we not mix'd like streams of meeting rivers,
Whose blended waters are no more distnquish'd,
But roll into the sea one common flood?

—Rowe

The 1954 light green Ford Coupe was parked right out in front of Erie Resistors Co., where I worked. It was a crisp October day, and the leaves had been falling for a couple of weeks now, past peak season. There were multiple shades of green and a variety of golden hues. The sharp red, wine, and cranberry colored leaves were now turning brown. The kaleidoscope season full of color was coming to an end. I love autumn.

As I got closer to the car, Ed smiled and opened the door. He looked at me and said, "Hey, something is missing from your hand!" I looked and asked, "What?" He pulled me closer to him and said, "Let me see your hand," as if he was kidding around with me.

Stormy Waters

He pulled me closer and then slipped on a diamond engagement ring—I was silent, stunned, excited, and honestly flattered. He caught me by surprise—it was like a bolt out of the blue. I looked down and saw the sparkle, the glow, and the glimmer of the diamond. I was breathless.

You know that doll you fantasized about as a child—the one that you thought about, dreamt about, and wanted for so long? Remember when finally, one Christmas morning, you saw a big box sitting under the tree? You ran to it with a look of glee, scrambling as you unwrapped it, and there she was, beautifully dressed in a floor-length gown with a train as long as a church aisle. She had crinolines, slips, and stockings, even a corset that made her look like a real debutant, and a long, long veil with detailed, scalloped lace on the edges that sailed down and over the train. There were those creamy colored pearls resting softly around her neck and sleek, high-heeled, satin shoes with cutouts and a bow on each of them. And the gown—it had pearls and stunning jewels that gleamed, one hundred twenty fabric-covered buttons down the back,

Past

and layers upon layers of silk organza fabric that just felt like heaven. There was even a blue garter belt and a plastic penny to put in her shoe. She looked like an elegant princess—enchanted and all dressed up for a glorious church wedding.

But now it was me; I was nineteen, and Eddie was serious—it wasn't a dream, it was real. I felt dazzled and charmed; I wanted to whirl around and dance. I felt as special as special can be. I was the prince's sweetheart.

Since you were a child, you have heard the tale of finding love—it's the Cinderella syndrome. You know those movies you watched and dreamed along with, starring all those gorgeous, magnificently dressed movie stars? Remember the sweet, lovely dresses your paper dolls wore, nestled safely in the box in the attic?

I must be dreaming . . . wake up . . . it's all a dream . . . But it wasn't a dream! It was my turn to walk down the aisle with my Prince Charming.

I looked up, grinning ear to ear and feeling so shy, and burst into tears and just hugged and hugged Eddie. I felt I was going to jump out of my skin as I exclaimed, "Yes! Yes! Yes!"

Stormy Waters

And so that was the beginning of our life—a milestone to say the least. It was October 20, 1960. On June 3, 1961, we were united for life as man and wife at St. John's Roman Catholic Church in Erie, Pennsylvania. Then we left for our honeymoon to Washington, D.C.

At the time, Ed was a second year college student. He started college after coming out of a four year stint in the Navy. He still had three years left to get his engineering degree. In those days, it took five years to graduate with an engineering degree.

In 1962, we were blessed. Our precious Denise Marie was born. In 1964, our beloved Therese Marie was born. After Ed graduated from Gannon University in 1964, we moved to New Jersey, where he got a job. Four years later, in 1968, came our adorable, darling Cheryl Ann.

Before we even had our third daughter, we knew one car wasn't going to do it. Ed bought a used TR4, which he continued to drive to and from work for fifteen years. He had to change the transmission twice over the years. Life was all a bed of roses.

Like heck it was. It was a struggle, especially being away from our families. It was very difficult for me because Ed traveled a lot. I missed my family desperately.

In 1965, Ed worked full time during the week and took a weekend job selling real estate. It was a real trek from

Past

New Jersey to Staten Island. It took a lot of stamina and determination, and he was always exhausted—he really wasn't cut out to be in sales. A year and a half went by, and that was the end of that.

In 1979, we bought a replica of a 1929 Mercedes Classic, which proved to be an endeavor that knocked Ed for a loop. It was tedious, costly, and almost beyond reach to complete. In all honesty, it took years. It always took the back burner to more important chores or situations. The fine-tuning and detailing were actually completed by my brother Tom. Hurrah for his patience and dedication to realizing Ed's dream.

Money was tight; raising three children put demands on both of us. I took a job as a seamstress for a fabric store. Shortly after that, I started my own drapery workroom. From there, I took courses and attended seminars, eventually to become an interior designer. At the same time, Ed took more college courses and traveled a great deal. Eventually, he started to work in the top secret department of the government. He had an organized mind, knew what he wanted out of life and where he wanted to go, and he wasn't afraid of the future. He always put me first and made me feel that we lived for each other. I was a headstrong and determined young woman. Ed always told me he was proud of my independence and achievements.

Ed was involved with the girls in their sports and school activities. He drove them to meets in Virginia, Delaware, and wherever else needed. He was the girls' confidant—he helped and comforted them with many issues. They loved him desperately and always knew they could go to him for anything. They were our pride and joy.

Ed continued to travel and work very hard, but working for the government was extremely taxing on the family. He was often gone on trips for meetings and presentations—Texas, Washington, and Panama, just to name a few—or commuting for hours back and forth to the Pentagon. Life had its ups and downs. As the time went by, we saw a little light at the end of the tunnel.

We were married twenty-five years before we had our first real vacation. Our three daughters completely surprised us by chipping in to give us a trip to St. Thomas in the Caribbean. What a marvelous surprise that was—we left on June 3, 1986. We were smitten by the Caribbean, to say the least, and bought a time-share at Bluebeard's Castle, which we still have.

Past

After college for the girls came graduations, new positions for the graduates, weddings, and then the most marvelous of all creations—our eldest, Denise, presented us with our first grandchild, Kaitlyn McKenzie, on August 30, 1992. We were delirious with joy. In 1995, our first grandson, Nicholas Edward—the "Imaginarium"— was born, followed by Heidi Lynn and Micaela Frances in 1997 and Greta Marie in 1998. We were so blessed. We were also thankful to inherit Jessica Lynn, Jonathan Richard, and Jake Scott through marriage.

Ed had a quiet presence, a gentle soul, and walked softly, yet he also had the energy of a true Renaissance man. I felt at times it was a lonely existence: on top of all that traveling, he couldn't share much about his work with me, or anyone else for that matter. Ed did call every single night while he was away, no exceptions, no matter where he was. He retired from Fort Monmouth in 1992. Then, after a year off in 1993, he started doing consulting work for three different corporations.

The challenge of flying and desire to do it never left Ed. He prided himself on completing his solo flight and getting his pilot license. That took many hours, and

Stormy Waters

squeezing them into his schedule was an accomplishment worthy of praise.

He was also always drawn to the sea, most likely because he had been a sailor for four years. He decided to take the test for a captain's license. We chartered boats on occasion and experienced the true sailor in Ed when he was at the wheel. Jibbing was a scream—knocking me back and forth as I dodged the sails to avoid hitting my head. We had so much fun.

Ed was in his fifties when he started to golf. His fondest memories and challenges involved golfing in the Henchel Golf Tournaments at the Oak Lane Country Club in Connecticut every summer with his son-in-law, Eddie. They even came in first place once.

I sit here and try to remember all of the interruptions and activities and trips to see our family that took priority over so many other projects we set out or wanted to do. Isn't that called "life"?

Life was full—the setbacks, disagreements, and disappointments were always forgotten due to memories of happiness and abundant blessings. The yearning or hunger for things unreachable turned to

Past

gratitude and satisfaction because we were always so happy to have each other. There is nothing about life on this planet that can measure up to the joy experienced in being loved.

After deciding to move into a senior community in 2000, we put our two-story colonial home on the market. A smaller home would give us more leisure time to relax, travel, and enjoy some of those pleasures we couldn't fit in before—especially spending more time with our grandchildren and families. We found a lovely nest in the southern part of New Jersey where the golf course was less than a mile away and the bay was less than three miles away. We were both very content with our choice. Ed planned to retire in September of 2001 while I continued my interior design work.

The lovely ranch-style home we chose sat on the corner lot; it had soft, buttery colored siding and toasted almond shutters. The sun poured in the south and west exposed windows, and it was away from the noise of hectic traffic. It was so planned with details, expectations, and beliefs of a new adventure. The anticipation, fulfillment, and charm of a new home invited us to look forward to a more

Stormy Waters

restful, peaceful environment. Sadly, it wasn't completed until after our *Lord* called Ed to Heaven to be with *Him*. Realizing and lamenting that Ed wouldn't be living there with me simultaneously sent me into orbit and left me immersed in grief.

Death leaves us with blind vision.

Leaves have their times to fall,
And flowers to wither at the north wind's breath,
And stars to see — but all,
Thou hast all seasons for thine own Death!

–Mrs. Hemans

Past

Remembering the Love

The wedding was lovely.
My heart stopped.
I feel the beat gone . . .
I can't feel.
I can't hear.
I can't breathe.
I can't believe it!
Until death,
Do us part . . .

Stormy Waters

The Touch of Joy

I hear a whisper,
I feel the brush
Of tenderness on my lips.
I hold tight while you hold me.
I know I've experienced more
Than that of some queens or duchesses.
The cry of joy sings out
Of the blazing glow in your eyes . . .
You love me.

Past

Hear Me Lord

The design of the body, as intrinsic as it is,
Can only function
When the stem cell
Is connected with you,
My Lord.

A Timeless Love

Your clever wit . . .
Your soft touch . . .
Your quiet walk . . .
Your late-night phone calls . . .
Your ever-loving care and concern . . .
Your outlook on life . . .
Your dedication to the girls . . .
As the years go by, Eddie,
I continue to recognize and realize
All that you were and all that you gave me.
None of it is material things.
It's your smile . . . the way you tilted your head.
It's the way you put your hand over your beard.
It's the dignity and wisdom you had.
It's the way you cuddled up to me.
It's the way you spoke . . . ever so softly.
It's your wisdom you shared.
It's your steadfastness that we loved.

Past

Your rare honesty . . .
Your simple, clean approach to things . . .
Your gentleness . . . your kindness . . .
Your love of building
Your classic car . . .
Driving your TR-4 for fifteen years,
And replacing two engines.
Your love for sailing . . .
Your love for golfing . . .
Your love for flying . . .
Your love for your children,
And grandchildren,
And sons-in-law . . .
Your love for theology . . .
Your fairness to all . . .
Your compassion and consideration . . .
Your knowledge and understanding . . .
Your undying love to me.
These memories are held in that secret place
So dear to my heart.

Stormy Waters

Fantasize

*I feel like a silly schoolgirl,
And I'm sixty . . . giddiness overcomes me.
Your senses wakened my sleep.
Your calm gives me peace and acceptance.
Hold me, let's sway with the wind.
Lord, help me sing and holler
With the joy I've lived.*

Past

Bond of Togetherness

I was Mrs.
I was one of two.
I was the other half.
We were meshed . . .
And we were one . . .
A unity of thoughts
Of ideas
Of goals
Of adventures . . .
What are we now?

One night, I got out of bed and
saw only half of me in the bathroom mirror.
Where was the other half?

Present

Mine after-life! What is mine after-life?
My day is clos'd! the gloom of night is come!
A hopeless darkness settles o'er my fate!

—Joanna Baillie

We felt an explosion of joy as we walked through our new home. The sun filtered in through the dusty, unwashed windows; the floors were covered with musty sawdust, nails, pieces of molding, and fixtures with their labels. Dust from the work in progress flew in when we opened the backdoor. It was Sunday, August 5, 2001.

We stood together in the open doorway looking out and around the property, examining the unfinished lawn, interior, and roadwork. As we held each other, Ed said, "This will be nice when it's finished." We giggled a bit and felt fulfilled with our choices, humble as they were. "Welcome to our new abode," he added. Neither of us mentioned our disappointment in all the delays with the builder.

Stormy Waters

On Wednesday, August 8, the furniture store had exactly what I was looking for—a pie-crust shaped, distressed cherry dining table with six chairs. *Boy, will Ed be in his glory*, I thought. *He loves dark wood.*

I signed the invoice and then got onto the parkway to North Jersey. Robin, my office manager, and I were going to look for area rugs for a client. No more than a half hour into our ride, my cell phone rang. It was Terri, my daughter. She said, "Mama, Daddy is in the hospital—hurry! We're at Riverview Hospital!" Robin offered to drive, but I turned the car around and sped—an unbelievable speed that couldn't separate reality from concern.

When I walked into the trauma area, Eddie looked okay. They said it could be the heat—102 degrees. He fell at work and had an aneurysm in the frontal lobe of his brain. Terri and I looked at the X-rays with the neurologist; Ed and I talked and visited. I stayed there, and all three girls came. He slept; he would wake and seem fine. Tests and more tests, doctors coming in and out—a cardiologist checked him, and Ed still seemed to be fine. He slept well that night. The next day involved additional tests and discussions—next we were told he may have congestive heart failure along with complications. A cloud of queries and issues were thrown in our faces one after another.

Present

Suddenly—"Mama! Mama! It's Daddy!" Denise ran as if in a triathlon, screaming, yelling, and crying. "Daddy is choking and not responding." We got there in a flash, surrounding Eddie. *What do I do?* I thought. *There's no room here. Drapes, nurses, assistants, equipment, and doctors—it's stifling. How can I help? What can I do?*

Finally, after what felt like forever, a doctor came up to me, pulled me aside, and said, "Pull back out of his line of vision; he will respond better. Stand over here by the drapes." The feelings of helplessness and inadequacy were overwhelming; I felt absolutely powerless. I stood like a frozen pipe while they worked on him. He choked and gasped and finally said, "OH *GOD!*" as loud as can be, and that was exactly where he went—to be with our *Lord.*

The bedlam just began. The fog set in as unanswered, haunting questions consumed me. No comment or answer was sufficient. The inexplicable was facing me, forcing me to believe the unbelievable. "Do you want an autopsy?" they asked.

Death is a new beginning, the presence of being with our *Lord,* but not for those left behind, and I was only one of them. Acceptance and belief were challenged by

Stormy Waters

my refusal to acknowledge what had happened. My daughters and I were seized with shock and disbelief. We were enraged, and our tears were uncontrollable in the trauma room. "Daddy . . . Daddy . . ." the girls said repeatedly. Where was my courage?

As the days, months, and years continued, my daughters and their families were living, walking, and talking saints. I fell into despair, and they took over everything. When I say everything—I mean everything. I was limp and nonresponsive, in a mental coma with a drastically fluctuating mood. I had, and sometimes still have, visions or dreamlike experiences drifting between the past and present.

I am in space somewhere—not flying, floating, or flailing—it is uninhabited, no conversation. I sense great music, art, literature, and beauty around me. I stretch and cannot touch a wall, the ground—nothing. I find a sense of rhythm, allowing my breathing to soften, and I don't even protest. I am just there in a certain place in space while the presence of serenity is within me . . .

The wind blew wisps of my hair, and it flipped and softly touched my face. Then a warm glow came over me

Present

as I experienced a conscious aroma of roses surrounding me; they were immeasurable in number. It was enticing and delightful and amazing to be alone in the midst of this beauty. The sizes and colors were astounding: each with a name tag—Queen Elizabeth, Best Prize, American Beauty, and Madame Butterfly. As I turned, I saw Silver Petals, truly a lavender color. They awoke me to the memory of our wedding—I had lavender roses made into bouquets for the bridesmaids.

As I was drinking in the variety of scents and hues, I looked down and saw millions of tulips—just like being in Holland. Suddenly, with a great force of wind came the most majestic bird I've ever seen—huge, with grandeur beyond belief. The feathers were a deep sable brown with touches of cloud white and caramel here and there. As I stared at it starry-eyed, one of the wings brushed ever so slightly on the tips of my fingers—I squirmed, unable to contain myself. I hadn't realized that he was that close to me, but his wingspan was that of an airplane.

He took over the sky; he soared, dipped, whirled, and turned down and then up. The bird was so graceful, gentle, strong, and gigantic—all at the same time; I was in awe. His command of the space took me to another level. I didn't tremble. I wasn't frightened. This massive bird had a force that left me supremely calm. As this

Stormy Waters

marvelous bird disappeared, he left a deep shadow that covered the sky.

I looked down and continued to gaze at those tulips. The mouths on these tulips were so big I started to think I could cuddle up in one of those delicious cups. They were daring me to come down and rest in their velvety smoothness.

In the stillness and calm, raindrops fell all around me. The flowers needed their nutrients and nourishment to grow strong, stand tall, and hold their own stature among the variety of blooms. As the luminous and soft colors of a rainbow covered the massive space, I felt my toes touch something—they were the most delicate, tiny buttercups and lilies of the valley.

While walking among these precious blossoms, I saw signs around me—signs of promise that persuaded me to follow them. I wanted to embrace these promises and claim their joy. The meadow nearby was so sensational and unbelievably fascinating. Mellowness surrounded my senses as the sun came out onto the cool water and sparkled and jumped on the soft ripples of the pond.

With great hesitation, I felt a strangeness I couldn't grasp. Everything stopped as my awareness went toward a flight of stairs. Slowly, with painstaking effort and feeling a sense of withdrawal, I wavered quietly, tiptoeing with restraint; a coolness came through me. With unconscious effort and struggling, I walked into a room and saw myself on the bed. I was lying hidden in a place where there was no beauty or scent of grandeur. It was me, *alone*, deep in the covers and pillows, bellowing. Then, in quiet murmurs, I was reaching across the bed with my arms for Eddie, feeling the loss and emptiness that took over. The awareness came like an icy wind in the summer heat.

Lord, give me faith and insight.

Prayer of Widows and Widowers
Author Unknown

Lord Jesus Christ, during *Your* earthly life, *You* showed compassion to those who had lost a loved one.

Turn *Your* compassionate eyes on me in my sorrow over the loss of my life's partner,

Fill this emptiness until we are together again in *Your* heavenly kingdom as a reward for our earthly service.

Stormy Waters

Help me to cope with my loss by relying on
You even more than before.

Teach me to adapt to the new conditions of my life
and to continue doing *Your* will.

Enable me to avoid withdrawing from
life and make me give myself to others more readily,

So that I may continue to live in *Your* grace
and to do the task that you have
laid out for me.

Erroneous, erroneous, erroneous. Life is full of erroneous tales with which we were raised. Who said we wanted this?

Sleeping alone.
Eating alone.
Walking into an empty house.
Driving alone in the car.
You're alone now!
"Sorry to hear about your loss!"
"Oh my *God*, I just heard!"
"I feel so sad for you!"
"How are you feeling?"

Present

"Take it easy, you'll be fine!"
"Try to not spend too much time alone!"
"Maybe you should see a counselor—that will help!"
"Did you ever hear how great those
bereavement classes are?"
Who is going to put my necklace and bracelet on?
Who is going to fix the flusher on the toilet,
adjust the pipes, and change the filter?
Oh *God*, how can I get through all this?

Shaken and distraught you find a way . . .

I wrote on scraps of papers, then a little spiral notebook, and finally in my journal when I misplaced everything else. What did the future hold for me? I honestly never thought about it. I took one moment, one minute, one hour, and one day at a time. I shuffled around in a dreamlike state as I tried to hold myself together. I slept and cried a lot, or was it I cried and slept a lot? You know that wall at the end of the hallway? I really wanted to bang my head into it just to get knocked out for relief from pain I couldn't reason with.

My daughters came often. Oh, how they felt the loss. Their emotions were drastically affected—they had such great ties to their father. I visited them, kept busy with the grandkids, and tried really hard to act normal, but the

Stormy Waters

sour face I wore was exasperating and embarrassing. I did go out to lunch and dinner on occasion with friends, though I wasn't myself.

Slowly, I began to believe in the prayers I was saying and beseeching of our *Lord*. It's not like a switch you use to turn on a light. It's more like when an old car repeatedly won't start, so you have to keep pushing on the pedal—and then what? You flood it. You have to wait and try again before it will start. What a relief. Then two weeks later, the same routine.

My girls were like lost souls in Siberia. Their husbands held them up when they were down. Every one of us continued with our jobs and tried to regain some composure and purpose in life again. Exhaustion and fatigue were overwhelming and upsetting; we were wounded souls. Our lives were upside down. We all wore different masks at different times in order to face the ongoing sorrow and disbelief. The pain wouldn't go away—neither would the reality of it. We were all fools thinking it would. We tried so hard; we pretended to accept his death, but with each occasion, birthday, anniversary, any holiday, we faked our way through it.

Present

That Christmas, only four months after Ed died, none of us could face having the holidays at our homes. Instead, we all went to a country inn in New Hampshire called The Dana Place. Despite being surrounded by such festive decorations, including five Christmas trees displayed in splendor, we cried and felt such undeniable grief.

Then the grandchildren, those little darlings of ours with those sweet little faces, showed us the true meaning of Christmas. They brought us out of our self-pity and encouraged everyone to gather around one of the trees in the library. We pulled ourselves together and opened Christmas presents, which brought joy, laughter, and happiness for the moment. Children are truly the saving grace in so many situations. After that, we gathered for an old-fashioned Christmas dinner. It was delicious, with an amazing variety of foods from yesteryear. From the outside, we looked like a happy crew; we did a good job of hiding our sorrows. With each upcoming season, our mood swings were less frequent, though revisiting old memories always brought waves of tears—an experience others have when they go through tumultuous times as well.

Stormy Waters

There were communions, confirmations, graduations, and even our granddaughter's wedding. Ed's face became fainter, and memories of him were stored deeper and deeper in our hearts.

The photographs and framed pictures we still have in our homes are such a comfort. We all want Eddie here to celebrate these milestones in our lives. But darn it—he's not here and there will always be those unexpected times when we break down. We go on and by the grace of *God*, life turns around as we go forward.

Let's open our arms joyfully to new beginnings.

Present

The End Has Come

I shook,
I shivered,
I choked.
I'm surrounded
By grief.
My body is absent,
My mind obscure.
My brothers
Frank and Tom held me up,
All the way to the altar.
I saw a box,
A structure,
The remains of my life,
Staring at me.
I wept,
And drifted in a cocoon.
I hid
In that shelter.

Death

Is this an injury?
A separation?
Am I in a capsule or a coma?
When will I reappear?
Lord, when?
When will meaning come back?

Present

Waves Wash Over Me

The white caps of the waves hit my feet,
I jump back.
I shrink – it's cold.
The sand is grainy and I sink.
The air is cold and lurks at my side.
The sky is grayer than I can ever
Remember it.
The noise is echoing in my ears,
I stand frozen in time . . .
Ohh! The fresh water awakens
And reverberates the tingling on my skin.
Lord, the cloud is rushing and overshadowing
Everything I knew!
My life has become bleak!

Stormy Waters

What to Feel

Flames – low, simmering flames . . .

So low you can hardly see them,

Yet they are there!

What's that smell?

Heat . . .

A scent!

An intrusion!

"Lord, I forgot to turn the burner on the stove off!"

The mind is a blank.

The body is there.

The emotions are torn.

Am I still standing there???

Present

Falling into Helplessness

I'm on the top of the extension ladder —
Right on the top rung.
I'm stuck . . . I can't go up . . . I can't go down . . .
I'm fallllllling . . . I'm fallllllling up . . .
No, I'm fallllllling down . . .
Help . . . help me. I'm here . . . No, I'm there . . .
I'm nowhere . . .
Where am I?

Body Within

Please get me out of here!
I'm being held prisoner!
In my own body!
Hurry!

Present

Links of Separation

I'm a domino.
We were dominoes.
We connected.
We linked.
We were separate but one.
And we were parted.
And they all fell
Down . . .

Confusion

The state of mind I'm in is
Certainly not one of the fifty we know of.
I know geographically I can't find it either.
It's cold, it's hot, it's barren, it's close.
It's empty.
It's far, it's crowded.
I don't even know which side of the equator
It's at.
I wouldn't advise anyone to go or be or visit.
It's empty and meaningless!

Present

Breaking into Pieces

The garbage disposal is on,
I'm being shredded,
Torn to pieces.
Nothing is left.
I disappeared!
Can I be retrieved?
Without a lot of physical damage . . .

Stormy Waters

Closing Down Inside

I'm choking!
I can't breathe!
The air is cut off.
What's happening to me?
Where did my other lung go?
Oh, Lord, you took him up to You.
How will I ever function!
I need oxygen . . .

Present

Lost in the Wilderness

Disconnected, detached.
Disoriented.
How do I get connected again?

Stormy Waters

Speaking into Silence

*Can't you hear me – all of you
out there?
In the cars, in the houses, in the
stores, on the streets?
Can't you hear me?
My husband died – he's gone!*

Present

The Question?

*Can I go on . . .
Without you?*

Falling Apart

Still shedding tears.
Crying should wash the soul.
You're on my mind, my heart, and inside of me.
My connection with you is constant.
Those tears of frustration are
Like waves swallowing me up.
I feel broken.
There are parts of me flying all over.
Where will they end up?

Present

Forgotten

The air is cool.
The leaves have turned
To prepare for a new season
The clocks have been set back
To start a new reason.
For those who need to rest
To begin the merriment
Of holidays to return.

And . . . here I am with no mention!

Stormy Waters

It's a hurricane.
A ferocious storm.
The water is shedding . . .
They're tears.
Tears of joy that you didn't suffer.
Tears of sorrow . . .
Tears of missing you!

Present

Stillness

*Be still . . . wait upon the Lord.
As I fidget and turn and tap my foot,
Knowing the contempt my emotions
Are going through . . .
Tick . . . tick . . . tick . . . tick . . .
I feel a nerve agitating me on my neck.
Lop . . . lop . . . lop . . .
I hear my thinking
In my ears.
It's a rage working on the very
Skeleton of my body.
Can anyone hear me?
I lost my soul mate . . .
I'm screaming!
I'm yelling!
I'm bellowing!
Can you please tell me you hear me!
Oh, Lord, You hear me don't You?
Touch me! Touch me!*

Stormy Waters

Appropriate Expectations You Can Have for Yourself in Grief
By Dr. Therese A. Rando*

Your grief will take longer than people think.

Your grief will take more energy than you would have ever imagined.

Your grief will involve many changes and be continually developing.

Your grief will show itself in all spheres of your life: psychological, social, and physical.

Your grief will depend upon how you perceive the loss.

You will grieve for many things both symbolic and tangible, not just the death alone.

You will grieve for what you have lost already and for what you have lost for the future.

Your grief will entail mourning not only for the actual person you lost but also for all the hopes, dreams, and

---

*Taken from: Rando, T. A. (1991). How to go on living when someone you love dies. New York: Bantam Books, pp. 79-80.

Present

unfulfilled expectations you held for and with that person, and for the needs that will go unmet because of the death.

Your grief will involve a wide variety of feelings and reactions, not solely those that are generally thought of as grief, such as depression and sadness.

The loss will resurrect old issues, feelings, and unresolved conflicts from the past.

You will have some identity confusion as a result of this major loss and the fact that you are experiencing reactions that may be quite different.

You may have a combination of anger and depression, such as irritability, frustration, annoyance, or intolerance.

You will feel some anger and guilt, or at least some manifestation of these emotions.

You may have a lack of self-concern.

You may experience grief spasms, acute upsurges of grief that occur suddenly with no warning.

Stormy Waters

*You will have trouble thinking
(memory, organization, and intellectual processing)
and making decisions.*

You may feel like you are going crazy.

*You may be obsessed with the death and preoccupied
with the deceased.*

*You may begin to search for meaning and may
question your religion and/or philosophy of life.*

*You may find yourself acting socially in ways that are
different from before.*

*You may find yourself having a number
of physical reactions.*

*You may find that there are dates, events, and stimuli
that bring upsurges of grief.*

*Society will have unrealistic expectations
about your mourning and may respond
inappropriately to you.*

*Certain experiences later in life may resurrect intense
grief for you temporarily.*

Present

The ice was here, the ice was there,
The ice was all around:
It crack'd and growl'd, and roar'd and howl'd,
Like noises in a swound!

— Coleridge

Sometimes I felt frozen solid inside a huge, massive chunk of ice. In my frozen state, it seemed like ice prongs were piercing into me. At first, the ice never seemed to melt. Thankfully, as time went on, the ice did melt, bringing relief, joy, happiness, and love for a new beginning.

Future

The deepest ice which ever froze
Can only o'er the surface close;
The living stream lies quick below,
And flow —and cannot cease to flow.

—Byron's "Parisina"

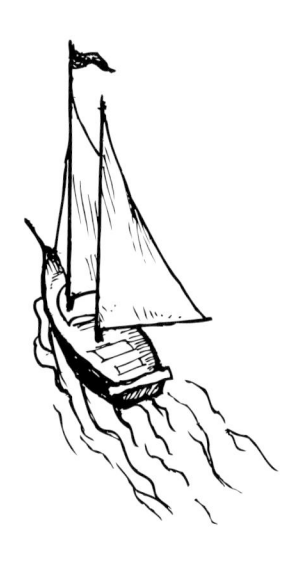

August 29, 2003

It's a most excitingly beautiful day outside. The sun is strong and glares with a beam that touches my heart.

Eddie, my love—I must stop mourning you and go forth. We have shared so much—such depth and beauty; I glow inside when I think of these times. I must tell you, my love, I have always been so very proud to have been your wife. I'd give anything to have a hug and a kiss, be held by you again, and lie next to you. Our heavens on earth have been many and glorious, and that's what gives me strength to go forward. My

Prince, as I remember the life we had together, I am so grateful for all that you have been to me.

I ask and beg and plead to our most gracious, loving God to continue to be so kind and generous to me. As I ponder and think of these years, my heart is full of gratitude and peace knowing that you are with our dear Lord. You left a mark on me that will tender my heart forever.

Eddie, we never did touch on or decide what life would be without each other. The agony and pain produced rage that contaminated my mind with grief and sorrow. The duration of the stormy waters was relentless. I know our Lord wanted you with Him, and knowing that my love for Him is so deep, I now know I'll be able to face a new beginning.

Through all the masks I've worn and the weeping and sadness I've incurred, our most merciful, comforting Lord has blessed me. I feel so undeserving, but, my Prince, when the agony got too great for me, God gave me His promises to hold on to. Tom recently entered my life; he, too, has lost his wife. We both have shared so much about our losses.

I've been thinking about how Jesus so eloquently loved us while he suffered and died for us. I am so thankful for His gift of love. Our Lord presented the possible for me with a new future, a renewed sense of being loved, and a strength that can endure the sweetness of a new life, which I believe He has in store for Tom and me.

In Scripture, David flees to "deep waters" (in Psalms 69:1, 2, and 14 and Proverbs 18:4 according to RBC Ministries). As we think of "water," it's not the water we drink from the faucet but the scriptural water—a water that will supply us so full of Him that all our needs will be met, all our wants satisfied, and all our thirst completely filled.

My love,
Keeks!

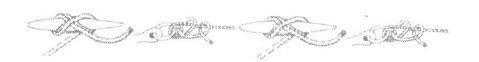

Like the swell of some sweet tune,
Morning arises into noon.
May glides onward into June.

—Henry Wadsworth Longfellow

Future

Alone, Alone, Alone Again

I close the door
I get into bed
I lie down
Alone!

Stormy Waters

Time Is Passing Me By

I find I can't quite grasp all of
Anything in life
It's this morning . . .
Then it's the next morning . . .
They come and go and I can't
Remember what I should remember
About those days as they pass.
The frustration of it all is a
Wilderness that I can't fathom.

Petition

Lord, do I have the right to ask
To have someone else near?
I don't want to be alone
Here!
I want the comfort and love
Again!
I want the company and someone
To hold me!
I want the love I had and that I hold
Dear to my heart!
Lord, teach me what you want!

Stormy Waters

Searching

*Lord, hug me.
I'm so lonely.
I miss my partner.
Who's going to love me?
Who's going to support me?
Who's going to accept all of me?
Who?*

Future

He Touched Me . . .

Every morning Mother Nature whispers . . .
"Strive . . . struggle . . ."
Every night her last message is "sleep."
Rest in the knowledge: "I am with You."
The struggles don't disappear . . .
We keep spinning . . .
But "Awe!"
Perseverance gives power to the weakness.
I know He's there . . .
I feel His nearness . . .
I believe He's
Touched me!

Stormy Waters

Thy heart is big, get thee apart and weep.
Passion, I see, is catching; for mine eyes,
Seeing those beads of sorrow stand in thine,
Began to water.

—William Shakespeare

Future

From Sorrow to Stillness

I am living in the rapids, Lord.
The sky is dark.
The clouds are burdened with
The weight of the heavy rain.
The sea is raging with unremitting
Torrents of crashing waves.
Behold!
Wait!
I see the soft drizzle falling on the
Settling waters.
It is flickers of light peaking through those
Deep purple, gray, dusty clouds.
The rays of sun are shimmering on the sea.
So delicate, the drips of rain
Look like they are dazzled and dancing
On the rippled waves that strokes and
Whispers — calmly!
"I am with you, and I am taking you
on a new journey."

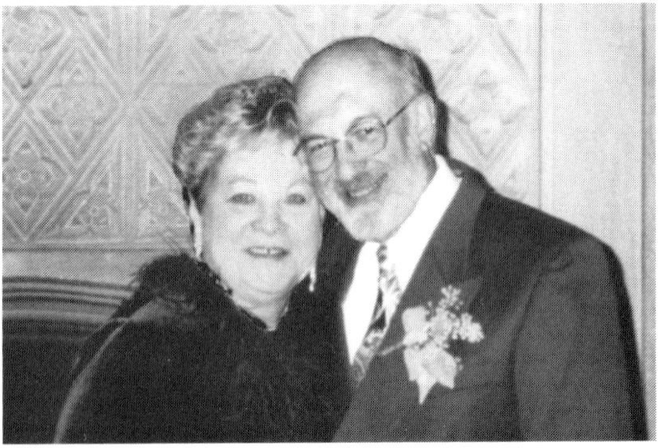

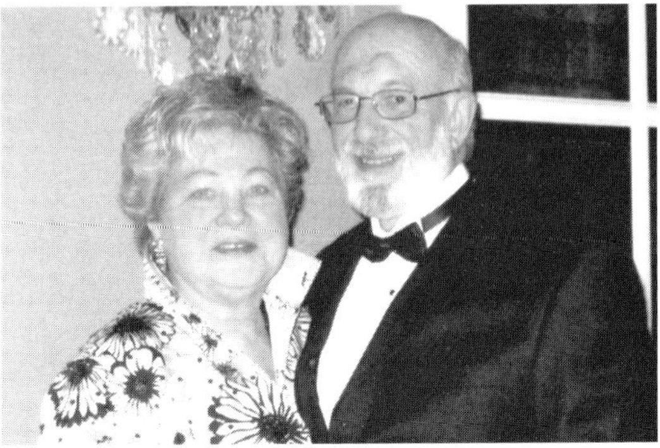

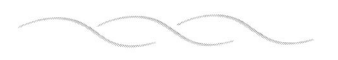

A Fairy Tale Romance

Once upon a time in a far away village, there lived an old princess who was very sad. She weeped and grieved all day and night, for her prince of forty-one years had died. She felt lost and devastated. In her grief, she turned to the *Lord* for guidance and solace. A long time passed, but she continued to weep and grieve. The *Lord* was her only comfort.

In another village far away, there lived an old knight who was also forlorn and distressed, for he, too, was experiencing similar pain. His wife of thirty-nine years had died, and in his grief, he didn't know where to turn. He knew there was something that could help him, but he didn't know it was our *Lord.*

Meanwhile, back in the first village, one of the princess's daughters saw how troubled her mother was. She worried and fretted, but she knew somewhere there must be an old knight looking for a princess.

Stormy Waters

Friends of the knight saw how troubled he was, and they, too, were concerned and didn't know where to turn.

After the daughter miraculously learned about this old knight, she thought about how wonderful it would be if this man could meet her mother. Maybe they could help each other. Maybe the *Lord* would work *His* wonders. With help from his friends and her daughter, the two met.

The old princess and old knight talked and talked and talked. They had much to say to each other, for they had a lot in common. As time went on, they realized they had similar interests . . .

What an adventure it became . . .

Over the hills and down the dales, they went together to strange lands and new places; they visited tinkers, tailors, and sailors, and surprise, surprise—a few New York gift shoppes along the way . . .

Behold, as time went by, the old lady and old man magically became young again . . . like young lovers with light hearts.

The families rejoiced, for they betrothed and lived happily ever after.

One True Knight

As days of chivalry seem to fade,
I remember one Knight and his chivalrous ways.
"True Tom" as his name, a tall, quiet man,
Who journeyed quite far over seas and over lands.
One day, he came to a kingdom by the sea,
Surprise, it was a maiden he did see.
Both Tom and the Maiden were waiting, you see,
Waiting for someone, their reason "to be."
Now as the tale goes, a bold test need be won.
The knight must pull forth a sword deep in a stone.
If he was the truest and kindest of hearts,
The sword would break free and a new
life they could start.
As Rosalie, the fair maiden, did gasp,
True Tom pulled the sword free with
one mighty blast!
And that is the tale of Rosalie's "True Knight,"
Together they'll be for each day and each night.

Stormy Waters

This old adage, written by my son-in-law, Rich Fergus, inspired the theme my girls used at the surprise Jack and Jill wedding shower for Tom and me. There was a huge papier-mâché stone and a replica of an old sword for Tom, my true knight, to pull out. It was an amazing experience.

Epilogue: There Is Hope

As a survivor, I've found life isn't anything like before. Yes, I do mean before Ed died. Those feelings of finality, abandonment, and desertion are only some of the emotions, queries, and sensations of unbalance and turbulencies of sorrow that don't go away for a long time—sometimes years.

A dear friend, daughters (in my case), or a spiritual advisor can help tremendously.

Meditation and prayer are mandatory for grief. Venting is a big part of going forward. Crying, lots of it, cleanses the soul.

There is no easy way to deal with loss—every person is unique and handles it differently. Part of us dies inside with the loss—be careful not to run from what sits on your plate.

Stormy Waters

Try to keep busy so you don't become obsessed. There are insurmountable chores, emotions, and tasks that seem to multiply as one day heaps piles onto the next day and the next and the next . . . then into weeks of oblivion. Weakness, uncontrollable suffering, and feeling forsaken take over.

We have clear images of the gifts and scenes from our shared past with our now lost loved one that will be with us forever. We feel such gratitude and warmth with these thoughts.

Hold tight. Force yourself—I mean it—FORCE YOURSELF to accept and face the death, and slowly, in dealing with each fear and anxiety, you'll be able to face a new hour . . . then a new morning, afternoon, and evening. Don't fool yourself into believing he or she is coming back. It's agonizing but true. This is where Scripture and leaning on our *Lord* bring calmness and insight.

Be in control of your feelings and emotions by eating properly. Take short walks. Self-understanding will help because each of us knows our own trigger areas. It is a process; as time goes on, we regain our strength and fall into the folds of a new life. Deep breathing and relaxing clear our heads and help us get a grip.

I could philosophize and give all kinds of advice and lists of dos and don'ts, but for some reason, nature sits in control of everything.

Epilogue

Our children and grandchildren are also going through all kinds of separation anxiety and searching unknown territories that are like being in the wilderness. You ache and hurt and want their pain to go away too. Consoling each other is part of the pain that is insurmountable; it's the sorrow that is staring us all in the face.

We grasp each moment and hold onto it for dear life as we suffer painfully at each stage of the healing process. Sulking, guilt, forgiveness, and pity are intensified and are all part of it. Reach deep inside and lean on your faith; it will never fail you. Close your eyes and create a blank in your head; concentrate on calm, peace, and serenity. It takes some practice, but it comes. Ask our *Lord* for direction and acceptance. Keep asking, don't give up . . . remember, *He* is always there for all your needs. Believe—believe and practice.

Investigate options for advice—call your church, a physician, a psychologist, bereavement groups, or others who have lost their spouses. Going out to shop, to see a movie (a good comedy so you can laugh), to the museum, or to art shows is an absolute reprieve. Writing letters, journaling, and reading grief books are excellent avenues for solace.

You're in a stage of unhappiness, and there will be times that no reassurance will help. It's a roller coaster

Stormy Waters

ride—you're up, you're down; one moment you're alive and fresh, then the next you plunge into guilt and resentment.

Turn the shower on and scream and cry; then relax in releasing some of those emotions. I've done it time and time again—unabashedly so, but it brought me cleansing and allowed healing to begin. Each of us finds our own path of recovery, and I believe you can too.

Each day as I open my eyes, I say, "*Lord*, where are you taking me today?" I must have said it thousands of times. Find a mantra that gives you great peace and grace.

Take one step at a time, put one foot in front of the other, thanking our *Lord* for all those blessings you incurred over the years and all the blessings he has in store for your future. Be grateful that *God* is so merciful; there is hope.

Believe me—all of your beautiful, rich memories will always hide deep in that secret place in your heart, along with the unsaid. It's a long, difficult process, but over time you will reach acceptance and feel a greater degree of calmness in your heart. You will find that as time passes, you have power over the sorrow, and the pain will ease up.

Epilogue

*You will experience rich, wonderful, treasured
moments and happiness again.
You will rebuild. You will laugh again.
You will have recovery and growth.
You will discover a new path.
You're going on a new journey.
You are strong.
You are cherished.
You are, and always will be, loved.*

Afterword: A Faith-Filled Journey through Grief to Hope

When a beautiful, soft, fuzzy, green-apple-colored caterpillar with its numerous short legs goes into its cocoon, oblivious to nature's own plan, it will eventually emerge as a magnificently beautiful butterfly. Each new creation is ready to fly, and each has a unique array of colors and design all its own. The butterfly is set free to seek nutrition from a variety of flowers.

This analogy illuminates the story of my own life, as well as my present husband's. We both knew true love and were devastated by the loss of our spouses. We developed a rare sense of concern for each other, and it blossomed into a rich array of experiences that are dear to our hearts. We learned from each other and gained

Stormy Waters

an incredible sense of direction as individuals and as a couple.

We've cried together, opened our hearts to each other, and started on a new adventure in life. We eased into it slowly; we had to heal individually before letting the process take its own course. We found that because we loved before and knew the essence of true love, it felt natural to love again.

Our love now in no way interferes with what we had before. Going forward was an adventure that is hard to describe. Our fluctuations between sorrow and happiness pulled us closer. No one could understand unless they traced our footsteps. We grew in understanding, patience, and concern, mostly wanting to find joy in life again.

We both knew our losses also affected our children. We hoped they knew and understood the realities of the circle of life.

I go back to my granddaughter's first Holy Communion party. At the time, Tom and I were dating. We were in the kitchen, and I put my hand on his back and rubbed his shoulder. The next thing I knew, all three of my girls were gone and in the bedroom crying. I found out that they couldn't deal with the fact that I touched Tom the way I used to touch their father. Moreover, Tom would put his hand on his beard and smooth it out, just like their

Afterword

father did. You see, going forward played a big role for my children too. Believe me—their pain was mine also.

Although time heals, it isn't always the same for each child. Each of my girls came around at a different time. Most interestingly, at some point each one came to me on her own and said, "Mama, I'm so happy you're happy; that means a lot." I knew then that their hearts were open to growth. I found it amazing that my girls understood the need for us to be a family versus their need to protect me or judge and challenge this change.

The girls love Tom dearly, but I don't fool myself. They have their own deep affections for their dad that cannot be touched and, believe me, there are times it's very difficult for them. I admire each of them for the continuous respect and honor they give to Tom. No one can take the place of their biological dad, but with an open mind and an understanding of deep love in their own marriages, my girls have come to a place where they see Tom as family. They are committed to my need to be loved and fulfilled. I cannot express my deep admiration, pride, and love for my daughters.

My husband Ed and I had unconditional love for each other and our girls. I know my girls saw that and instilled the same unconditional love in their own lives. I believe that's why they were able to see a new future for me. They

Stormy Waters

put me and my feelings for this new course in my life first. Although Tom is not like their father, they recognized the gentleness and generosity of Tom's spirit. There isn't anything they could bring to Tom that he wouldn't help them with. There is, after five years of marriage, a bond and a connection between Tom, my girls, and their families. The grandchildren are crazy about him too.

We have found that love conquers everything. Life is beautiful and full of unexpected joys. The future holds an immense amount of happiness; many of the promises of our *Lord* have come our way. We pray together about these promises. Our love is genuine. We still have our moments of grief and sorrow; however, because we both understand, it's easier to comfort each other. The toughest times are always the anniversaries of our previous spouses passing, which bring up old memories that will always be part of our hearts.

There is no easy solution for life's unexpected issues; we just work through them—that's the real answer to a great life together. Try as we may, there are problems and circumstances each new day that sneak up on us, just like they do for everyone else. Our secret to handling them is turning to our *Lord* for his support and direction. We found we can't do it alone. I guess we are human, and our *Lord* wants us to keep humble and teach us to lean on

Afterword

Him. God is at work, even in the midst of the problems and frustrations of our day. I believe *He* alone is sovereign—that is why I can trust *Him*, even when the way seems impossible at times.

I lived in a cocoon for some time after Ed's death, and it wasn't a happy place. I felt like the caterpillar, racing around inside the cocoon with multiple legs, even though none could help get me out. One day, I realized I can't do anything about things that I'm not meant to solve. Leaning on the Serenity Prayer, as I have for some time, brought me peace. Prayer and more prayer is what our *Lord* wanted from me. Just like the butterfly that emerged out of its cocoon, I emerged from mine.

Tom is a chemist and a fisherman. He's as busy as I am with my design work and this book. Oh yes, our families make life hectic too. We have found a new life together—and yes, it's colorful and full of unexpected events, rich with travel and fun but with setbacks. The design of our life is up to our *Lord*. We look forward to many new adventures and happy times on this journey.

> *We are afloat over the deep waters, but we trust the sea to keep us buoyant.*

——— Memories ———

Stormy Waters

Rosalie and Ed got engaged on October 20, 1960.

Memories

From left to right: Bill Rhodes, Patti Straub, Sylvia O'Mally, Nancy Benedict, Tom Osiecki, Judy Osiecki, Dan Stolinski, Tom Czulewicz, and David Czulewicz.

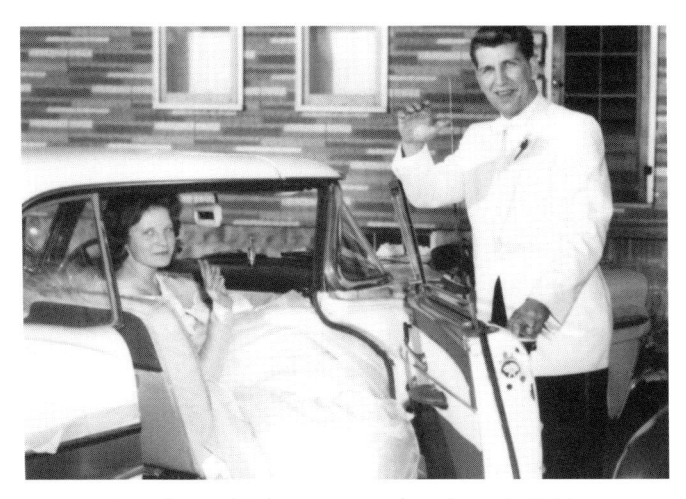

Rosalie and Ed got married on June 3, 1961.

Stormy Waters

Our daughters: Therese, Cheryl Ann, and Denise.

Rosalie and Ed on a chartered boat in St. Michaels, Maryland.

Memories

Cheryl and Ed.

Ed and Therese.

Left to right: Therese, Ed, Rosalie, Denise, and Cheryl.

Stormy Waters

Ed's replica of a 1929 Mercedes.

Greta, Micaela, and Heidi on their trip to Niagra Falls.

Memories

The Walsh family: Jessica, Eddie, Jonathan, Denise, and Kaitlyn.

Jonathan, Kaitlyn, and Jessica Walsh in 2008.

Stormy Waters

Left to right from top: Rich, Jake, and Cheryl Parker, Nicholas and Micaela Parker Semanchik.

Denise, Jonathan, and Eddie Walsh at Jonathan's graduation from Northeastern.

Memories

Married couple Matt and Jessica.

Nicholas, Jake, and Micaela at Christmas 2008.

Our family celebrating Christmas at The Dana Place in 2001.

Stormy Waters

Top left: Heidi at a horse show.
Top right: Micaela and her horse Cheyanne at a horse show.
Bottom: Greta getting ready for a horse lesson.

Memories

After seven years, we honored Ed's wishes for a Viking funeral. The girls didn't want to part with his ashes, so they each took turns with the urn. We agreed that Ed needed to be put to the sea and on August 9, 2008, we gave him a sea burial.

Back row: Tom, Rich, Eddie, Rosalie, Rich, Cheryl, Nicholas, Jessica, and Matt. Front Row: Jonathan, Denise, Micaela, Greta, Heidi, Jake, Kaitlyn, and Therese.

About the Author

Rosalie Czulewicz married Edward Stolinski Jr. in 1961. During their forty-one years of marriage, they raised three children, who gave them eight grandchildren.

Rosalie currently owns and manages Interiors by Rosalie, an interior design firm with both residential and commercial clients along the East Coast.

Rosalie lives in Little Egg Harbor, New Jersey, with her husband of five years, Tom, the "knight" who swept her off her feet in 2004. Together, Rosalie and Tom have helped each other through the darkness of grief and onward to the light of hope. They enjoy celebrating their love and life together through traveling.

Both the spontaneous writing of her poetry and the deliberate molding of this book contributed to Rosalie's healing process. She hopes that her faith-filled journey through grief to hope will inspire you no matter where you are, even in the midst of stormy waters.